Creativity

Discover How To Unlock Your Creative Genius And Release The Power Within

By Ace McCloud
Copyright © 2014

Disclaimer

Table of Contents

DEDICATED TO THOSE WHO ARE PLAYING THE GAME OF LIFE TO

WIN

KEEP ON PUSHING AND NEVER GIVE UP!

Ace McCloud

Be sure to check out my website for all my Books and Audio books.

www.AcesEbooks.com

Introduction

I want to thank you and congratulate you for buying the book: "Creativity: Discover How To Unlock Your Creative Genius And Release The Power Within."

Have you ever felt tired, drained of energy and completely bored? Have you ever had trouble mastering your problem solving skills, thinking differently, or finding inspiration for a project? Do you find yourself wanting to be more *creative* but can't seem to get the creative juices flowing on a regular basis?

Creativity is present in each and every one of us. However, some people are better able to naturally master it than others. We all have that friend who we describe as "so creative." Now, you can be that way too! If you are already creative, then there are things you can do to be inspired and bring that creativity out on a much more regular basis. Everybody has the ability to tap into their own unique creativity to think outside the box and bring truly unique and innovative ideas and projects into the world. All you have to do is learn how to tap into *your own* inner creativity.

One of the most common mistakes that people make when it comes to trying to improve upon their creativity is that they try too hard. Trying too hard can be very discouraging, especially when you don't come up with an answer or solution right away. Luckily for you, this book contains proven steps and strategies on how to naturally and easily bring out the creative genius that's inside you.

The key to tapping into your inner creativity is to separate the unconscious and conscious decisions of your brain while discovering how to combine them at the right place and time to create something great. This book will show you how to do this along with other creativity boosting strategies. You will learn everything you need to know about creativity and what you have to do in order to master it and bring it about in your life on a regular basis.

Keep on reading to discover how to tap into your own creative juices and potentially create something that can change the world as well. You will learn how to overcome common barriers to creativity and how to tap into habits that are great for boosting it. You will read about successful creative geniuses who have already left their mark on the world and discover helpful videos, interactive exercises, inspirational quotes and much more that will assist you in your new journey towards unlocking the creative genius with in you! It is my hope that you will use the information in this book to regularly nourish your creativity so that you will be inspired to go out and create something incredible!

Chapter 1: The Power of Creativity

Creativity has been a hot social topic during the past couple of decades. You have probably heard people talking about it in several contexts. You've probably heard somebody say that the children of today aren't creative anymore. Maybe you've heard someone say that the future of this world depends on creativity. Many people believe that parents and teachers should value it more and encourage it more often. Well, what exactly is creativity and why is it so important?

The general definition of creativity is to create or improve upon something with an original idea. Creativity is what has made many of your favorite movies, books, songs, TV shows, paintings, and sculptures. Creativity is also what helps create innovative new products and unique, successful businesses. It also plays a part in sciences, economics, cognitive psychology, and many other fields and disciplines. Creativity is intangible and it can be spread and shared all throughout the world. It is what keeps the world evolving. Some would say that creativity is what keeps life fun. Without creativity, the world would be missing many of the incredible breakthroughs that have transformed our lives for the better in so many ways.

Creativity is a natural process. Everybody has the ability to be creative, especially as young children. Children tend to have active imaginations and show it during their playtime. Think back to when you were a child—did you use your imagination a lot? Many of us have played house, pretended we were superheroes, used our toys in different contexts, communicated our visions through drawing, and more.

However, many people tend to lose hold of their creativity as they mature into adulthood. When you are distracted by things such as having to work a job, pay your bills, take care of a household, etc, being creative and using your imagination can fall to the wayside. Also, when you're older and you have to take care of certain responsibilities, you may have to sacrifice your passions for more practical things. For example, you might have been a great artist when you were younger but you decided to pursue a career in accounting because you knew you'd have a better chance at making more money. When that happens, you also pose a higher chance of becoming disconnected from your creative thinking skills.

The good news is that anybody can tap back into their creative abilities, no matter how long it has been. While it may seem hard, it's actually pretty easy and fun, when you know what to do!

Let's take a brief look at how being creative can benefit you today.

The Benefits of Creativity

Creativity Can Help You Solve Problems Better. When you have mastered the art of being able to use your creative thinking skills, it can in turn improve your ability to become a better problem solver. There is no instructional guide to creation, so it helps your brain get in a better habit of thinking independently and confidently.

Creativity Helps You Get Involved and Meet Others. When you create something and you want to share it with the world (or maybe just your local community, for starters), you have the opportunity to connect with others who share your same ideals. You also have the opportunity to exchange feedback with other creators. Finally, you stand a higher chance of helping others, especially if your creation is useful and practical. Even if you just write a small book, it could help others escape from their own realities or help them solve some important problems.

Creativity Can Help You Save Money. You've probably never heard of this one before, but it's true. Research shows that when you're better able to express yourself, your chances of making impulse purchases can dramatically decrease. As an added benefit, creating something can help you feel more fulfilled, unlike making an impulse buy. So, by being creative, you can save money and feel great about yourself at the same time.

Creativity Can Help You Establish Self-Awareness. Being creative can help you gain a better and more fulfilling sense of self-awareness. When you create, you tend to explore your thoughts and beliefs more deeply. This can lead you to better understand yourself, your habits, your needs, and your wants. In turn, this can also help you express yourself better.

Creativity Grants You Freedom. When you create something of your own, you're in charge. Unlike your job, where you've probably got to follow a set of rules and standards, anything is possible when you create, hence giving you a sense of freedom. There is no right or wrong way to create something of your own. This can help you get into the habit of risk-taking and opportunity-grabbing.

Creativity Can Keep You Healthy. Creativity can help you improve your physical and mental health. When you create something, you tend to become happier and more resilient. You may also feel a reduction in anxiety. Creativity can also help combat mental stress. Research has shown that people who report being stressed out tend to have weight issues, higher glucose levels, more upper respiratory problems, and a higher chance of developing heart disease. By being creative, you can help yourself become less stressed out and anxious, therefore limiting your chances of developing some physical problems.

Creativity Can Help You Stay On Track In Life. Creativity also tends to give you an idea of your life's purpose—without it, you may feel emptier inside.

When you're feeling empty inside, your chances of trying to fill the void with fake friends, materialism, medication, alcohol and drugs highly increases.

A Brief History of Creativity

As you have just learned, creativity can bring many benefits to your life. People have been practicing creativity for centuries. The concept of it extends as far back as Ancient Greece. At that time, the idea of art was meant to free oneself from "rules," just as it is used today. Those who engaged in creating artwork were regarded as having a vast and inspirational imagination. During the times of Medieval Christianity, the word "create" had a religious meaning: to create from nothing, just as God had done in the bible. Creativity was also a hot topic of the Renaissance period. Art and writing, specifically poetry, were all soon regarded as creative activities and not a craft.

Creativity Today

Today, the concept of creativity has truly developed. Whether you know it or not, everybody is creative today—it shows in the way you dress, in the way that you speak, in the way that you think, and much more. These small, creative, everyday things are what make you unique.

Creativity is what changes the world. When a person comes up with a new, useful, and/or helpful idea, something new happens in the world. When the inventor of the clap-activated lamp turned the idea into a reality, it saved many elderly people from having to get up to switch their lights on and off. When the creator of Pokemon, a card game that was extremely popular among children in the late 90's, was a small child, he liked to collect bugs. He essentially turned his passion into a huge industry. Creativity is what invented your computer, your car, your kitchen gadgets, and much more. Creativity is what creates successful businesses, industries, inventions, and events.

Chapter 2: How to Identify a Lack of Creativity

Anybody can be creative. Some people believe that they were born with creative personalities while others find it hard to take a step back from reality. Later on in this book, you will get the opportunity to participate in some exercises to help you tap into your inner creative genius. However, there is one major personality trait that can kill creativity in a flash, and that is having a huge ego. This chapter will take a look at how your ego can affect your ability to be creative. It will also outline some of the most common creativity killers and how to avoid them. Knowing these creativity killers is important for being able to tap into your creative skills later on.

Egos and Creativity

People who have big egos may find it harder to tap into a state of creativity because they are not flexible. They often find it difficult to step away from their comfort zone and incur small, personal risks that would fully allow them to connect with their creative endeavors. Creativity requires experimenting, risk-taking, and exploring unfamiliar grounds. People with huge egos tend to be afraid of doing any exploring for fear that they might discover their limits. These types of people often display certain personality traits. This chapter will take a look at some of the personality traits of people who tend to have huge egos. By knowing how to identify these traits, you can use this knowledge in helping to overcome mental creative blocks.

Victimizing Yourself. When you victimize yourself, you essentially give up and refuse to explore alternative options to a problem. For example, you may have had an argument over the rules of a game when you were a child. If you were the type of person who said, "Whatever, I'm just going to go play by myself," you essentially victimized yourself. The habit of victimizing yourself tends to follow many people into adulthood. When you're used to being a victim, it negatively affects your ability to be creative. You may not realize it, but in your mind, you're saying to yourself, "Oh nobody is going to appreciate my efforts so I will not focus as much as I should on my project." To overcome this personality trait, if you think you have it, you must learn how to identify the thoughts and words that put you into "victim mode." Whenever you hear them in your head or about to come out of your mouth, stop yourself and reevaluate your situation.

Defending Your Specialty. Another sign that you might have a huge ego is if you have a talent or a sense of expertise in a certain field but you do not allow others to share the spotlight with you. If you find yourself calling other people "amateurs" or harshly criticizing their works or ideas, you risk the chance of losing opportunities for collaboration, networking, and more. It can also make you look arrogant. When working or talking with others who have similar interests with you, make sure you understand the difference between having confidence and being to defensive.

Taking Critiques Personally. If you are the type of person who tends to turn everything said to you into an insult, you may also have a hard time boosting your creativity skills. By viewing criticism, comments, or remarks about your ideas and projects personally, you will only be wasting time that you could be spending on creativity. It is also harder to collaborate with others, because some people may even be afraid to say anything to you, in fear that you will take it too personally. If you find yourself having a hard time handling criticism, try to think of ways that you could use it to improve.

More Common Creativity Killers

Aside from your ego, there are several more common creativity killers that may be currently plaguing your ability to be creative. You may already be aware of some of these killers and you may actually be surprised by others. Be sure to pay good attention to this list so that you can be as creative as possible in life.

Find Your Role. Exploring different creative fields is important, but to be the most successful and productive person possible, it is important to find a field in which you excel. As Einstein once said, if a fish tries to climb a tree it will live out the rest of its life feeling dumb. Figure out what you're good at, what your talent is and what your strengths are and apply them to your life. This can be extremely difficult and sometimes you may have to search for years or decades, but once you find your sweet spot, your life will be so much better.

Restrictions That Are Too Deep. In Chapter 3, you will read about how placing restrictions on yourself can actually boost creativity. However, some restrictions can actually kill your creativity. For example, if everybody tries to go "by the book" at your job, that does not leave much room for your imagination. Another example would be if your boss did not allow anybody to suggest any new ideas. Get into the habit of being able to identify restrictions that may actually inhibit creativity and avoid them as much as possible.

Give Yourself Enough Time. Part of the creative process requires looking at one end-result from multiple angles, which will often require a good deal of thinking. A good deal of thinking often requires a good deal of time. Do not leave your projects to the last minute, especially if you have a deadline, otherwise the end result may come out rushed and unoriginal. By preparing ahead of time, it gives your brain time to mull things over and come up with original ideas or great solutions.

Have Diverse Friends. While you shouldn't pick your friends solely based on diversity, it is a good idea to try and become friendly with people who are different from you. Research actually shows that people who are alike get along well but they tend to be less creative. When you have the opportunity to make a new friend, try to identify what is different about them. You may end up collaborating with each other in the future, which could result in a great, creative end-result.

Hearing No Positive Feedback.   Criticism is important for helping you improve in areas that you may not have been previously strong in but hearing positive feedback about your projects is important too. Without hearing positive feedback, you pose a higher chance of giving up once you've hit the first obstacle. To increase your chances of gaining more positive feedback, put your works and ideas out there. There are plenty of online forums that specialize in art, writing, inventing, and many other fields that you could connect with people on. If someone in your life is always trying to put you down or be negative about what you are passionate about, be sure to limit your exposure to them or sit them down and let them know that they are not being helpful.

Chapter 3: Creative Habits to Boost Your Creativity

Now that you have learned a little about the common things that can serve as roadblocks to your creative abilities, it is now time to learn how to boost them! Finally, this process will start to get a little more fun. Again, some of these tips and strategies may be obvious to you but others may also come as a surprise. For the best results, try to implement all of these strategies into your life to become as creative as you can. However, you may need to experiment and see which ones work for you best. It will be different for everyone—that is part of being creative and unique!

Great Creative Habits

Tap Into Your Inner Strength. To become more innovative, it is important to tap into your spirituality and listen to what you have to say. Cut off any outside speculation from friends and family members and focus on your own thoughts. Often times you might look to others for support, but when it comes to creativity, your best source of support is from yourself.

Believe in Your Idea. People who come up with new ideas often feel self-conscious about them or they are afraid of being judged. When that happens, their creativity tends to crash. To be able to create something to your best ability, you should believe in yourself and in your idea. One good way to reinforce your belief in yourself and your ideas is to make a declaration. Stand in front of a mirror, put your hand over your heart, and say, "I can and I will create this."

Keep Learning. To be creative is to create something new but many people can become inspired by knowledge that already exists. Remember, nobody is ever too old to learn something new. Read books, listen to audio recordings, watch educational shows, search the internet, do whatever it takes to keep absorbing new knowledge. This is extremely helpful in stimulating your creative thought process. Some of the biggest fools on this planet are those who think they are so smart that they have nothing new to learn. The smarter you become, the more you realize that knowledge and the possibilities are endless.

Pay Attention to Detail. When you pay attention to details, you face a higher chance of living in the present moment. When you're living in the present, your world tends to become more loud and interactive, which can be very helpful in becoming creative. When you begin to notice small details about things, you tend to feel more inspirational and thoughtful. By paying attention to details, you can also get into the mindset of looking at things from a different angle, which can also be helpful in stimulating your creativity.

Channel Out Negativity. Many creative ideas never even get put down on paper due to negative feedback. While feedback is important for *improving* your idea, you should try to tune out all downright negative comments. One of the most common comments that kills peoples' creativity is, "It can't be done."

Don't Be a Perfectionist. When it comes to working on your project, try not to be a perfectionist the first couple times around. When you first start to work on your idea, let go of any mental stress and trust in your instincts to guide your pen, your fingers, your paintbrush, your thoughts, or whatever tools you are using to be creative. Once you've created something you're passionate and proud of, you can go back and perfect it later. This is extremely important to do, as the creating part of your brain is different from your editing or perfecting part of your brain. So, things will flow much smoother when you are just focusing on one or the other.

Have a Mantra. By picking out a mantra that strongly influences you; you can increase your chances of feeling and being creative dramatically. A good example of a mantra is picking a quote by a famous person who shares your creative field. So, for example, if you were trying to write a new song, pick an inspirational quote by a successful musician and repeat it to yourself to help you. It can also be something you come up with yourself that pertains to exactly what you are trying to accomplish. Try and fill your conscious thoughts with this mantra so that it increases your motivation and creativity and helps block out any negative thoughts that may try to creep in. For example, if you are a writer, a good mantra to repeat to yourself often could be something like: "I am an excellent writer and great thoughts and ideas come easily to me." Or simply the phrase: "I am a super creative genius."

Embrace Failure. As with any endeavor, some of your creative projects might fall through, never to get completed, or they may even be a complete flop. Don't be afraid of failure because, often times, you will fail. Look at your failures as a way to make a better attempt next time or improve on your next project. Sometimes you can even create something out of failure. I am sure you have heard this a thousand times before, but being able to build up an unstoppable belief in yourself along with persistence, there is almost nothing you can't accomplish if you just steadfastly work towards your goal, not allowing any failures along the way to stop you. This has always been one of my great keys to success. Once I have something that I am determined to get or attain, I will just move towards this goal with ruthless abandon. Long after the majority of people will have given up, I will continue to pursue my goals until they are a reality. Once you are no longer afraid of failure, the sky is the limit. If you do find yourself being fearful or anxious a lot, be sure to check out my bestselling book on Overcoming Fear.

Set Restrictions. Setting restrictions for yourself creates a challenge in itself, which can inspire you to think of creative ways around the obstacle. This is how Dr. Suess ended up writing the bestseller *Green Eggs and Ham* after betting someone that he couldn't write a story within a certain word-count. If you're a writer, challenge yourself to write a 500-word story if you're used to writing

2,000-word stories. If you're an artist, challenge yourself to draw something in 30 minutes instead of an hour. Whatever type of project you're working on or field that you're working in, set a restriction for yourself and see how it affects your creative thinking.

Try New Things. Many times it is extremely easy to get caught up in the same old routine of doing things. It is vitally important to try out new strategies, ideas, and techniques to find out what works best for you. If you find something that works well, be sure to write it down and come up with creative ways to utilize it in your everyday life. Maybe you always try to be creative at night after work, but experimenting in the morning for 30 minutes at the beginning of the day may lead to some great results. Maybe there are certain foods or supplements that get your creative juices flowing, and others that dampen them. Maybe certain types of music really stimulate you, or maybe being outdoors for a bit helps your thought processes. Be sure to catalog all this. If you find yourself in a "Flow" state of mind, being highly creative and productive and getting a lot of great things done, be sure to write down all the things that you did that day, what foods you ate, did you exercise, how much sleep did you get, etc. After a month of doing this, you should be able to come up with a great game plan for what works best for you to get those creative juices flowing.

Getting in the mood or the "Flow" State. Once you have figured out what works well for you, it is time to put it into action. For long term success, it is critical to be able to get your creative juices flowing on a regular basis. This is easier said than done, but those who can do it will have a huge advantage in whatever they do. I have personally found that one of the number one things that is extremely helpful when trying to perform at creative and peak performance levels is a healthy diet along with regular exercise. I won't go into great detail on this here, but if you want advanced knowledge on how to do this, be sure to check out my hit series: Ultimate Health Secrets and Ultimate Energy. Some other things have helped me personally is reading positive and informative books and information, listening to great music, a clean and enjoyable environment, engaging in exciting games or hobbies, nice plant life, being outdoors, juicing, using lots of healthy supplements, sunshine, getting plenty of sleep, aroma therapy, listening to audio soundtracks like the creativity booster from Hypnosis Downloads, surrounding myself with positive and uplifting people, proper goal setting, and regularly doing positive affirmations. It also helps to get yourself Motivated and Inspired towards what you are trying to accomplish and then exerting the self-discipline to follow through.

Daydream. Once you've started a project, allow yourself to daydream a little bit. Daydreaming has been shown to invoke the incubation of ideas. Don't limit yourself, just use your imagination to the fullest and have some fun with it. Some of the greatest people in all of history have been dreamers. If something comes up that you really enjoy or gets you excited, see if you can find a way to integrate this into your project or life.

Have Fun. Don't forget to have fun! Many creative people tend to find being creative fun already but it can be fun for anybody who gives it a try. It allows you to step back from reality and tap into an imaginary world—an escape—for a while. And the cool thing is, once you are done with this escape, you may come back with some incredible ideas and inspiration that will keep you motivated to work hard towards your goals.

Inspiration. Most importantly, when inspiration hits, act on it immediately! When the creative juices are flowing and you're feeling motivated and excited, do something to make your idea a reality. While it may seem like this feeling will last forever, it never does. So it is vitally critical to put everything else in your life on the back burner and get some serious work done based on your creative impulses!

Chapter 4: Successful Creative Geniuses

As you learned in Chapter 1, people have been practicing creativity since the times of Ancient Greece. Over the centuries and years, there have been many successful people who have been regarded as creative geniuses. These people have created great things, influenced the world while they were alive, and continue to influence the world after their death. These people are great role models to study and model yourself after if you're trying to accomplish great results for yourself. This chapter will take a look at some of the most famous creative geniuses in history and in the present day today. You will also discover how to identify a creative personality. As you will see, many of the creative geniuses that you will read about in this chapter have similar traits.

How to Identify a Creative Personality

Since creativity is such a powerful force, researchers have often looked at the personality traits of creative people. As a result, they were able to find some common similarities. This section aims to teach you how to better identify a creative person, both in others and yourself. These personality traits will allow you to get a better sense of who is creative and who isn't. You can also share this list with your friends and family to measure each other's creativity.

Here are some of the most common personality traits of a creative person:

Energetic, Yet Quiet. Creative people tend to be full of energy. They focus that energy into their projects as they concentrate and work long hours on it. As a result, creative people tend to be quiet and reserved. The energy they focus into their projects often generates a feeling of refreshment and inspiration. Creative people tend to have a good sense of control over their energy.

A Combination of Playful and Disciplined. Many creative people tend to have light, silly attitudes. However, they will work all night on their creative venture if they have to. Creative people tend to have a natural desire to be persistent in their work. To put it simply, creative people love to have fun, but when it comes to their work, they know how to get serious.

Having a Strong Imagination. Creative people tend to have a strong imagination and the ability to get in touch with it. People who are not creative by nature have a more difficult time accepting that their imagination can somehow be turned into a reality.

Introverted AND Extroverted. Creative peopled often possess both introverted and extroverted personalities. At times they are drawn to interacting with large groups and at other times they are drawn to observing large groups.

Proud Yet Humble. Many creative people are not arrogant or conceited. In fact, often times they are humble and modest about their works while displaying pride at the same time. One reason for this may be that they have quickly moved on to a new creative endeavor and are no longer interested in the last one.

Passionate Yet Objective. Creative people tend to be passionate by nature because creation requires passion. However, they are also very objective of their works, always open to criticism and improvement. Creative people want their projects to be memorable and credible.

Successful Creative Icons

Leonardo Da Vinci. Leonardo Da Vinci was a versatile Renaissance man who excelled in sculpting, painting, writing, making music, and inventing, among many more creative activities. Over time, many people have described him as having an amazing imagination. His best known creative painting is the famously known *Mona Lisa* followed by *The Last Supper*. He is also best known for his ideas on humanist theories. As a young child, Da Vinci did not receive a formal education or have many memories. During his teenage years, he worked with a mentor named Verrocchio as an artist's apprentice. While working with Verrocchio on the painting *The Baptism of Christ,* Da Vinci's talent for painting was discovered. For centuries after his death, Leonardo Da Vinci has been regarded as one of the most talented men in the world. Children all over the world read about him in their history and art classes. Leonardo Da Vinci's works and ideas continue to influence modern day art.

Vincent Van Gogh. Vincent Van Gogh was a famous Dutch painter whose works continue to make an impact on art today. Van Gogh's works are best known for having strong colors and emotional hues. As a young child, Van Gogh loved to draw. As he aged into his twenties, he began to paint some of his most famous paintings. All in all, he created 2,100 pieces of art. One of his greatest paintings is his *Self-Portrait with Straw Hat*. His other famous works include *The Starry Night* and *Wheatfield with Crows*. Van Gogh's most notable personal traits were a sense of seriousness and resilience. Most of his works were inspired by the bright works of Impressionists and Post-Impressionists. Many of his works possess strong brush strokes, which are thought to be inspired by his emotions. One of the most famous things about Van Gogh is that he was never recognized for his artwork until after he died—he only sold one painting while he was alive. Before his death, Van Gogh struggled with several mental health issues and ultimately took his own life.

Wintston Churchill. Winston Churchill was a famously known British politician who was also a writer, artist, and historian. As a young child, he was known to be rebellious and independent. He was often punished for his poor performance in school. Despite his strong career in politics and the government, Winston Churchill also participated in many creative endeavors. He was inspired to paint to ease his depression. He began to write for magazines and newspapers to earn extra money. He famously wrote several books that discussed ideas that were unconsidered weird, such as one idea to turn icebergs into aircraft carriers.

Mozart. Wolfgang Amadeus Mozart was a famous musician who was known for his talents by a very early age. Growing up in the 1700s, Mozart displayed a talent for playing two instruments by the age of five. By 17, he was employed as a court musician. Feeling unfulfilled with his life, Mozart began to travel. He eventually went to Vienna, where he composed some of his best concertos, symphonies, and operas. Some of his most famous works include *Symphony No. 40, Piano Concerto No. 24,* and *Don Giovanni.* Mozart was inspired by his father, who was also a musician, and also by the works of Bach. Mozart died from a sudden illness, right in the middle of composing *The Requiem.* However, Mozart's music still continues to inspire and influence modern music today—his classic works are appreciated by people everywhere and modern-day musicians have even remixed them.

Stories About Successful Creative Inventions

Some of the items that you have and consume today are results of creative inventions. Almost every aspect about these products, from their names to the way they were invented, are the result of creative endeavors. Here are a couple of stories behind some well-known, everyday products:

The Invention of Potato Chips. The story of how potato chips, one of the most popular snacks in America, was invented is actually a very interesting tale. One day, a man named George Crum, who was a chef at a restaurant in Saratoga Springs, New York received an order for French fries. The person who had ordered the fries sent them back, complaining that they were cut too thick. Crum cut them thinner and sent them back but the diner was still unhappy. In a creative attempt to aggravate the annoying customer, Crum cut them so thin that they would be horrible French fries. Surprisingly, the diner loved them and they eventually became known as potato chips.

The Invention of the iPod. Before the era of Apple and its popular iPod line, people had to carry their music around on cassettes and CDs. Cassettes only held a certain amount of songs and did not have the ability to skip through songs without experimenting with the fast forward button. CDs were an improvement and could sometimes hold more songs but the devices to play them in were bulky and the surface of the CDs could get easily scratched. While many people look to Steve Jobs as the inventor of the iPod, the idea actually came from Tony Fadell, a hardware engineer with Apple who wanted a better way to organize digital music. Together with Apple and the latest technology, the iPod was born. The name "iPod" was inspired by the doors of the spaceship in the move *2001: A Space Odyssey*.

Chapter 5: Release the Creative Genius Within You

Now that you have learned about the benefits of creativity, how to avoid becoming uncreative, and how to boost your creative abilities, it is time to put your brain to the test. In this chapter, you will get to test out your creative abilities. Here, you will find 10 exercises to try. Each exercise works a different part of your brain but can ultimately help you flex out your creative thinking skills.

Exercise #1: Learn a Different Perspective

This exercise was originally developed in 1967 by J.P. Guilford. The object of this exercise is to get your brain into the habit of viewing things from a different perspective, which can often get your creative juices flowing. The best thing about this exercise is that you can practice anywhere—at home, at work, while you're out to eat, while you're at a friend's house, etc.

For this exercise, all you need to do is look around your surroundings, find an everyday object (it can be anything—a plate, a bucket, a box, a picture frame, etc) and take two minutes to brainstorm as many ideas as you can on how you could use that object. For example, if you picked a paperclip, you could use it to hold papers together, to reset electronics, or you could use it to mark a page in a book. You could think of ways in your head but writing them down is often a better strategy because you will then have a visual aid.

This exercise can help you become more creative because it puts your thinking skills to the test. It measures how fluid, original, flexible, and elaborate your train of thought can be.

Exercise #2: Drawing From Figures

This exercise was also originally developed in the 1960's by Ellis Paul Torrance. The object of this exercise is to test your creative thinking by taking an incomplete shape and turning it into a more complete drawing. For this exercise, take out a few blank pieces of paper and a pen. On one of the pieces of paper, draw a basic arch shape that is slightly slanted to the right. On another piece of paper, draw the letter M but rotated on its left side. Then, take a few minutes and start making a drawing out of the original shapes. This exercise helps you flex your creative muscles and was originally used as an alternative IQ test. Feel free to modify the original starting shapes and then come up with your own unique drawings.

Exercise #3: Solving Riddles

When you were younger, you probably heard riddles amongst your friends. Riddles are tricky questions that require some creative thinking to come up with an answer. To test out your creative thinking skills, solve some riddles and try to figure out what the answer is. Here are some riddles that you can start with:

Riddle 1: The Thompson family consists of 7 sisters. There is one brother for each sister. Counting their Dad, how many males are there in the Thompson family?

Riddle 2: A frog fell into a 32-foot deep well. The frog jumped up the wall 2 feet every day and fell down one foot every night. How many days did it take him to get out?

Riddle 3: Andrea and Sue were born on the same day in the same month of the same year. They both share the same parents. They are not twins. How is it possible?

Riddle 4: Can a man marry the sister of his widow?

Riddle 5: Professor Crowley, an aging professor whose mind is also starting to age, passed through a red light and walked the wrong way down a one-way on his way to class. A cop saw everything but did nothing. How could that happen?

Answers:
Riddle1: 2—Mr. Thompson and the one brother to everyone.
Riddle 2: 31 days—don't count when the frog jumped out.
Riddle 3: they're part of a set of triplets.
Riddle 4: no because if he has a widow that means the man is dead.
Riddle 5: the professor was walking.

These are a just a few of the great riddles that exist out there. Keep your eyes and ears open for more. Solving riddles helps your creativity flow by testing your convergent thinking skills. For some more riddles that you can try solving, check out this YouTube video by Saif Ahamed Masood 25 Tricky Riddles with Answers.

Exercise #4: Word Associations

The word association exercise is a test in which you look at three words and then try to connect each one with the same word. For example, you could use the word "star" to associate with the words "falling," "dust," and "movie." People usually attribute a beam of insight to finding the solutions.

Here are a few word association sets to try out:

End-Shelf-Read

Death-Magic-Board

Row-Show Keel

Stomach-Home-Sea

Sweeper-Main-Walker

Answers:

1) Book
2) Black
3) Boat
4) Sick
5) Street

Exercise #5: The Candle Problem

The Candle Problem is a commonly used puzzle created by Karl Duncker, a psychologist from 1945. This puzzle is another test of creative problem solving skills. The object of this exercise is to get your brain to try and figure out how to use common items in unique ways.

In the Candle Problem, you have in front of you a candle, a small box of thumbtacks, and a book of matches. Your job is to figure out a way to attach the candle to a wall so that the wax won't drip on to the floor.

Solution: Empty the box of tacks, place the candle in the box, tack the box to the wall, and then light the candle.

For a visual of this problem as well as an explanation of this puzzle's significance and what motivates people to figure it out, check out this YouTube video, The Candle Problem, by LucideaStudio.

Exercise #6: Rebranding

This exercise allows you to really test out your imagination skills. Imagine that you are a marketing director and your first assignment is to redesign a brand that already exists. This exercise is flexible because you can pick the activity based on your interests. For example, if you don't like a product logo, get out some paper and design a new one. If you don't like a commercial, rewrite the script. This exercise can be very fun for practicing your talents and thinking of new ideas.

Exercise #6: Write a 6-Word Story

Writers will especially love this one. The challenge to write a 6-story word originated when Earnest Hemingway, one of the world's most established writers, was put up to it. His 6-word complete story was about baby shoes. Try this challenge out for yourself and see what you can come up with.

Exercise #7: Invent Something New

You've probably seen pictures of genius ideas passed around on your social media pages. Personally, I've seen creative ideas for baking, making alcoholic drinks, and simple tricks and tips to make life "easier" such as making ice cubes out of coffee to put in iced coffee. Look around you, think about the little annoyances that pop up in your life, and try to see if you can invent a way to fix it. You never know—your idea could possibly make you a millionaire if it works!

Exercise #8: What If

For this simple exercise, test out your creative thinking skills by simply brainstorming "what if" scenarios. For example, Stephen Spielberg said "What if dinosaurs ruled the earth?" and soon came the movie Jurassic Park. This is a good exercise for creative writers who are looking to come up with new story ideas. It's also good for aspiring inventors who can think of new and useful ideas for products.

Exercise #9: Revisit Childhood Fun

Young children tend to have the best imaginations. Without much subjection to judgment and criticism, their ability to be creative also shines through. For this exercise, take some time and allow yourself to do what you enjoyed doing as a child...play with some blocks, put on a costume, have fun with some action figures, color with crayons, etc. and see what your mind does. It can be interesting to see how your adult mind reacts to the creative activities that you liked to do as a child. Some potential questions that you can ask yourself while doing this exercise are, "How can these activities influence my career," and "How can these activities influence my personal life today?"

Exercise #10: Creative Binural Beats

Binural beats are music tracks that are able to directly affect your brain and state of mind due to the frequencies and signals of each track. Research on binural beats have found that your brain will respond to each beat, which can help induce certain activity, based on the nature of the track. For the best results, you should listen to these tracks in a dark, quiet, and peaceful area with headphones so that you can fully concentrate.

Here are some examples of binural beats that are thought to be able to stimulate creativity:

Binural Beats #1

Binural Beats #2

Binural Beats #3

Binural Beats #4

Binural Beats #5

After listening to one or more of these tracks, work on a project and see if it helps you create anything new. You should never listen to these tracks while driving. Individual results after listening to these tracks may differ. Do some experimenting and see which one works best for you.

Chapter 6: Inspiring Creativity Quotes

As this book comes to an end, I would like to share some of the best quotes on creativity that have been said by some of the most successful people in the field of creativity. These quotes are a combination of quotes from history and quotes from modern-day people. I hope they are able to inspire you to take some action and to use your creative abilities daily.

Creativity Quotes

"Every child is an artist, the problem is staying an artist when you grow up." - Pablo Picasso

"If you hear a voice within you say, *'You cannot paint,'* then by all means paint, and that voice will be silenced." - Vincent Van Gogh

"Have no fear of perfection, you'll never reach it." - Salvador Dali

"Curiosity about life in all of its aspects, I think, is still the secret of great creative people." - Leo Burnett

"You can't wait for inspiration, you have to go after it with a club." - Jack London

"Imagination is the beginning of creation. You imagine what you desire, you will what you imagine, and at last, you create what you will." - George Bernard Shaw

"Creativity is more than just being different. Anybody can plan weird; that's easy. What's hard is to be as simple as Bach. Making the simple, awesomely simple, that's creativity." - Charles Mingus

"Originality is nothing but judicious imitation." - Voltaire

"Creativity comes from a conflict of ideas." - Donatella Versace

"Don't think. Thinking is the enemy of creativity. It's self-conscious, and anything self-conscious is lousy. You can't try to do things. You simply must do things." - Ray Bradbury

"Creativity is just connecting things. When you ask creative people how they did something, they feel a little guilty because they didn't really do it, they just saw something. It seemed obvious to them after a while." - Steve Jobs

"You see things; and you say, 'Why?' But I dream things that never were; and I say, 'Why not?'" - George Bernard Shaw

"Creativity is contagious, pass it on." - Albert Einstein

"Creativity is allowing yourself to make mistakes. Art is knowing which ones to keep." - Scott Adams

"Creativity is a great motivator because it makes people interested in what they are doing. Creativity gives hope that there can be a worthwhile idea. Creativity gives the possibility of some sort of achievement to everyone. Creativity makes life more fun and more interesting." - Edward de Bono

"There is a fountain of youth: it is your mind, your talents, the creativity you bring to your life and the lives of people you love. When you learn to tap this source, you will truly have defeated age." - Sophia Loren

"Creativity takes courage." - Henri Matisse

"You see a child play, and it is so close to seeing an artist paint, for in play a child says things without uttering a word. You can see how he solves his problems. You can also see what's wrong. Young children, especially, have enormous creativity, and whatever's in them rises to the surface in free play." - Erik Erikson

"Negativity is the enemy of creativity." - David Lynch

"A hunch is creativity trying to tell you something." - Frank Capra

"Living creatively is really important to maintain throughout your life. And living creatively doesn't mean only artistic creativity, although that's part of it. It means being yourself, not just complying with the wishes of other people." - Matt Groening

Conclusion

I hope this book was able to help you to tap into your creative abilities and make them stronger.

The next step is to use what you've learned in this book and start actively practicing your creative thinking skills. Once you've gotten the hang of it, take any ideas that you come up with and turn them into a reality—even if you just take small steps to start. Start writing the first chapter of a book. Start painting the outline of a new piece of artwork. Start the blueprints for a new and useful invention. Whatever idea it is that you have come up with, don't forget to make it happen—that is the beauty of creativity. Don't worry about what other people may say or think, follow your passion. You may be amazed at what you are able to come up with and create!

Finally, if you discovered at least one thing that has helped you or that you think would be beneficial to someone else, be sure to take a few seconds to easily post a quick positive review. As an author, your positive feedback is desperately needed. Your highly valuable five star reviews are like a river of golden joy flowing through a sunny forest of mighty trees and beautiful flowers! *To do your good deed in making the world a better place by helping others with your valuable insight, just leave a nice review.*

My Other Books and Audio Books
www.AcesEbooks.com

Health Books

ULTIMATE HEALTH SECRETS

HEALTH

Strategies For Dieting, Eating Healthy, Exercising,
Losing Weight, The Mediterranean Diet,
Strength Training, And All About Vitamins,
Minerals, And Supplements

Ace McCloud

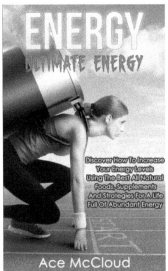

ENERGY
ULTIMATE ENERGY

Discover How To Increase
Your Energy Levels
Using The Best All Natural
Foods, Supplements
And Strategies For A Life
Full Of Abundant Energy

Ace McCloud

RECIPE BOOK

The Best Food Recipes
That Are Delicious, Healthy,
Great For Energy And Easy To Make

Ace McCloud

MASSAGE THERAPY

TRIGGER POINT THERAPY
ACUPRESSURE THERAPY
Learn The Best Techniques For
Optimum Pain Relief And Relaxation

Ace McCloud

LOSE WEIGHT

THE TOP 100 BEST WAYS
TO LOSE WEIGHT QUICKLY AND HEALTHILY

Ace McCloud

FATIGUE
OVERCOME CHRONIC FATIGUE

Discover How To Energize
Your Body & Mind So
That You Can Bring
The Energy & Passion
Back Into Your Life

Ace McCloud

Peak Performance Books

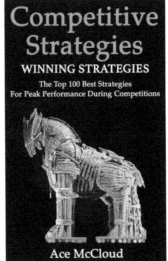

Be sure to check out my audio books as well!

Check out my website at: www.AcesEbooks.com for a complete list of all of my books and high quality audio books. I enjoy bringing you the best knowledge in the world and wish you the best in using this information to make your journey through life better and more enjoyable! **Best of luck to you!**

CPSIA information can be obtained
at www.ICGtesting.com
Printed in the USA
LVHW061514040422
715247LV00005B/227

9 781640 480179